S--THOLE Countries

Donald Gorbach

ISBN-10 1984026852
ISBN-13 978-1984026859

"WHY WOULD KIM JUNG-UN INSULT ME
BY CALLING ME 'OLD' WHEN I WOULD NEVER
CALL HIM 'SHORT AND FAT.'
OH WELL, I TRY SO HARD TO BE HIS FRIEND…"

—DONALD TRUMP

African Nations

El Salvador

Haiti